Silence Is Complicity

SILENCE IS COMPLICITY

A call to let teachers improve our schools

through action research — not NCLB

TORIN M. FINSER, PH.D.

STEINERBOOKS

2007

STEINERBOOKS

www.steinerbooks.org

AN IMPRINT OF ANTHROPOSOPHIC PRESS, INC.

610 Main Street, Suite 1

Great Barrington, MA, 01230

COVER AND BOOK DESIGN: WILLIAM (JENS) JENSEN

LIBRARY OF CONGRESS CATALOGING-IN-PUBLICATION DATA

Finser, Torin M., 1956–
  Silence is complicity : a call to let teachers improve our schools
through action research—not NCLB / Torin M. Finser
    p. cm.
  Includes bibliographical references.
  ISBN 978-0-88010-580-4
  1. Action research in education—United States. 2. Education—
Standards—United States. I. Title.

LB1028.24.F56 2007
370.7'2—dc22

                                                2007006630

CONTENTS

INTRODUCTION

AT A TEACHERS' conference in Oslo, Norway, held March 16–18, 2007, I was asked to give several keynote speeches on teacher research. I jumped at the opportunity, fully supported by Dr. Caruso, our new President at Antioch University New England, not only because of the chance to explore a new country, but also because I have long been an advocate for teacher research. Starting with our summer sequence program for experienced educators in 1992, I have taught regular courses at the university level that prepare teachers for Master-level projects and review research methodology. That led to the publication of a small pamphlet on research brought out by the Association of Waldorf Schools in 1995. With the confluence of that original piece going out of print and the exciting invitation to speak in Oslo, I decided it was time to edit and supplement the original work. With the permission of AWSNA and the continued support of everyone at SteinerBooks, I am able now to offer this new volume.

As I began to prepare for Oslo, I asked the organizers, "What prompted this conference on research and what are some of the current themes in independent Norwegian schools today?" What I heard really caught my attention. Apparently, the sixty Waldorf schools in that country have received government support for many years. Lately, the Norwegian government has passed legislation calling for the "lifting of knowledge" in which the schools are being asked to clarify competencies and aims of each subject taught, with demonstrations and descriptions required for achievement at ages 9, 12, 16, 17, 18, and 19. Minimum standards needed to be articulated and much paper work was required. In addition, the government has been asking for descriptions of "quality care" in administrative matters, parent relations, decision making and other practical matters.

As I listened, I realized why they had asked an American to speak at their conference! Those of us in education on this side of the Atlantic, and even many who are not working with schools, have been debating our own set of standards, passed some years ago and known as "No Child Left Behind" (NCLB). The Norwegian situation at once appeared, if not similar, at least the beginning of the same trend. But their response intrigued me! Rather than just comply, they called for a large conference to look at alternative ways to improve the quality of education. Rather than just follow the new regulations, they have suggested that teacher research might serve as an alternative pathway to standardization, especially if it were to be rigorously embraced, monitored and subject to peer review. This got me all fired up. Here were teachers willing to do the extra work to push back, so to speak, in the face of government regulation of education. Rather than complain and blog one another, these teachers, by attending such a conference and taking up action research, could make a difference in the whole tenor of the public debate. Here was an example for those of us who have been concerned and complaining about our own problems with NCLB and unfunded state mandates in general.

This leads me then to make my basic case for teacher research:

1. When conducted according to accepted quantitative or qualitative methods, teacher research can help teachers learn, develop new curricula and stay enthusiastic about the discovery process. There are immediate, tangible benefits for both teachers and students in action research.

2. When successful, teacher research can serve to empower teachers in their advocacy for educational change. With firsthand experience and earned knowledge, teachers can more confidently speak out for the needs of their students. Those in other professions, such as medicine, engineering and business, are often afforded greater respect and compensation than teachers who have to endure countless commission reports and political debate about what others think should be happening in our schools. It would be great for a change if the voices of teachers were heard in our public discourse! They work with children everyday; they know what materials and curricula are needed, if only they were left alone to follow their instincts. Teacher research takes this beyond intuitive understanding to a level of documented inquiry that could be held up for public scrutiny, such as in publications,

news media, workshops and town meetings. Teachers need a greater voice in educational matters!

3. Given the enhanced curriculum and stronger advocacy on the part of teachers, we might achieve a third aim, which would be to get politicians to back off. No other professional field is so regulated and legislated as is education. Somehow, someone got the idea that in a democracy everyone has an equal say in educational matters. Yet when I go to the dentist or doctor, they are comparatively free to perform their work according to standards set by their professional organizations. I have yet to read a newspaper article describing legislation mandating a certain number of fillings per week before a dentist is publicly labeled as "failing." Yet we seem to have no problem letting politicians set very specific standards and test scores for our children. Teacher research, if followed as described in the book, could create a counter movement that would be so dynamic that parents and community members might band together in a popular revolt that essentially said: Politicians, back off!

This will of course take time. But I sense that more and more people are willing to follow the lead of Jonathan Kozol (author of *Savage Inequalities* and other books) in challenging common mis-practices in funding, testing and legislating. Most social change happens when people start to speak out and others rally to the cause. The time is right for such a surge in regard to educational reform.

So I introduce this modest booklet, which seeks to frame some of the key issues in the first two chapters and then take the reader in a step-by-step approach to making research a viable option for teachers. Having coached countless students over the past fifteen years with their Master-level projects and having served on doctoral committees at several universities, I have been able to hone the techniques described here based upon life experience. Repeatedly, students and teachers have said to me that the research experience has been transformational. They have not only learned to become better teachers and stronger advocates for what they believe, but they also feel their lives have changed as they follow a question that becomes a steady companion on the journey of teaching. Research, as indicated toward the end of this work, is not just about outcomes and school reform. It is an opportunity for awakening, for inner development. In this regard, there are truly no limits to knowledge—no boundaries around personal growth.

1. STANDARDS SET BY THE FEDERAL GOVERNMENT: WHO HAS BEEN LEFT BEHIND?

SOMETIME DURING THE 2007–2008 session, Congress must determine whether to renew or amend the No Child Left Behind Act (NCLB) or leave it to expire. As the public debate progresses, there will be opportunities not only to question specific provisions but also some of the fundamental premises built into the original resolution. With the benefit of several years of experience, thoughtful teachers, parents and administrators have already begun to offer their views. In this chapter I will offer some of the thinking from this group as well as some of the key ideas that prompted the legislation in the first place.

From the outset, the assumptions behind NCLB were controversial:

1. Virtually all children, even those living in poverty, have the capacity to achieve a preset level of proficiency in reading and math by the age of eighteen—and it is the teacher's job to make sure they do.
2. Everyone benefits from having someone look over his shoulder, and that external pressure

from the government/accountability improves performance.

3. Good education is synonymous with good teaching, thus NCLB required tighter standards in teacher licensing such as "highly qualified teacher" designations.

4. Giving parents choices within the system has positive benefits as competitive pressures force educators to customize programs.

5. Improving education is a national imperative, and "the federal government can and should play a constructive role."[1]

Some studies have shown limited success in the narrow sense of occasional improvements in test scores, but the evidence is what one might call "underwhelming." For example, the Education Policy Analysis Archives cites a two-year study of NCLB in southwestern Washington State based upon drop-in observations in classrooms and interviews with teachers and administrators. The data indicated that the policy had "partially yielded the intended standards-based reforms but at considerable local cost. While most participating administrators described efforts to use NCLB to leverage needed change, most teachers described struggles to sustain best practices and to avoid some negative consequences to their students and schools."[2]   Administrators reported that some resistant teachers were being "nudged" out of the profession, and that the greatest attrition was at the fourth grade level where the tests were being administered.

Indeed, most of the teacher response I have surveyed has been neutral to negative. Some of the most frequently voiced objections are as follows:

1. There is increasing evidence that schools are turning into test-prep factories and the curriculum offered as a result is narrowing.

2. In the pursuit of reading and math scores, the overall breadth and depth of the curriculum has diminished. Learning is being sacrificed at the expense of skill development.

3. The parental choice aspect has not panned out. For example, NCLB cannot solve the problem that in some big cities there simply are too few good schools to choose from—the government is incapable of quickly conjuring up new, successful schools.

4. The federal government has always had a hard time forcing states and local governments to do things they don't want to do, and even if they go through the motions, it's nearly impossible to force them to do those things well. As with children, they have to want to succeed.

5. Speaking of children, many teachers have reported that over-reliance on testing has reinforced a student's tendency to ask: Will this be on the test? Then they devalue anything that is not. Ironically, some studies have shown (Popham 2006) that most of the tests used under NCLB are "unable to detect any striking instructional improvements when such improvements occur."[3]

6. Poor students and students of color are not improving, and they are the ones most likely to be taught by inexperienced teachers.

7. By requiring that teachers demonstrate subject matter competence in each subject that they teach, NCLB not only recognizes the importance of subject matter knowledge, but is forcing out middle school teachers in rural schools who have to teach several subjects as part of full-time job requirements. Subject area expertise is being pushed at the expense of the overall generalist and a more integrated curriculum.

8. The notion of "failing schools" is a form of public ostracism harking back to the "scarlet letter" condemnations that used public opinion as a punitive weapon. Embarrassment and ridicule do not promote growth and change.

The most significant questioning in my view concerns the very role of government in setting standards in the first place. Even some of those who have been NCLB advocates in the past are making statements such as these by Mike Petrilli on what to do now: "In my opinion, the way forward starts with a more realistic assessment of what the federal government can reasonably hope to achieve in education. Using sticks and carrots to tug and prod states and districts in desired directions has proven unworkable."[4]

He suggests the federal government's role should be restricted to distributing funds and collecting and publishing data, leaving everything else in the "don't do it at all" bucket: "No more prescriptive 'cascade of sanctions' for failing schools. No more federal guarantee of school choice for children not being well served. The states would worry about how to define and achieve greater teacher quality (or better, teacher effectiveness). The states would decide when and how to intervene in failing schools."[5]

So it seems that NCLB has resulted in some sincere questioning of the role of the federal government in education. Shifting responsibility to the states has the virtue of more local control (at least in states such as New Hampshire) but does not eliminate by any means the role of government in education, a premise I would like to more thoroughly question in chapter two. One has to wonder if the same arguments Petrilli uses to question the federal government forcing unwanted changes on states should not be applied to states doing the same to local districts. Can excellence in education be legislated at all?

One crucial issue is the notion of setting standards and forcing schools nationwide to achieve them. Government does not do this for business, for if it did, entrepreneurship would seriously suffer. Imagine legislation that would mandate five percent profit margins for shoe stores or fifteen percent for technology, and then publicly brand companies as failures if they did not achieve these preset standards. As a society, we tend to value free enterprise and individual creativity in business but not in education, and we do this at our peril.

One of the main problems is the setting of standards in the first place. In her book *One Size Fits Few*, Susan Ohanian asserts that the Standardistos have de-professionalized teaching:

> How else are teachers to feel except helpless in the face of being told to *deliver* a curriculum that is invented by external authorities? Nationwide, we have the lowest retention rate of teachers in history.... What few people realize is that there is

no *reform* in the Standardistos documents: Standardistos are trying to pass off macaroni and cheese skills as *Ziti con Formaggio Velveeta di Alfa Romeo* gourmet dining. They want to perpetuate the same old skill drill that kids have been resisting all this century.[6]

Teachers are caught in the bind between best practices known to most dedicated educators and the generalized arrogance of standards such as these issued by the Illinois State Board of Education:

Every elementary school child will be able to read at grade level, with fluency and comprehension.

Every elementary school teacher will be able to teach reading using comprehensive, research based methods.[7]

And these and other standards are to be applied to all students regardless of their experiential background, capabilities, developmental and learning differences, interests and ambitions. These standards are intended for students in districts with ample resources *and* those that cannot even afford school supplies and lab equipment. The brush of standards tends to paint all schools with an unexciting, oppressive hue of gray. Real people otherwise known as children and teachers become numbers and charts. Standards set outside of the teaching profession are detrimental to all learning and creativity.

It is amazing, as stated previously, that only in education do people feel it legitimate to have outsiders set predetermined standards of achievement. Does the government legislate how many operations a surgeon should perform per week? Does anyone outside of the industry decide how many innovations a technology company should adopt in a given year? Did anyone require that Picasso produce a certain number of masterpieces a month demonstrating proficiency in certain techniques? The surgeon, painter or inventor relies upon the very human capacities that good teachers are trying to cultivate in our schools. These qualities include such things as imagination, critical thinking, problem solving, interpersonal skills, creativity—most of which are not valued or measurable on any standardized test. In focusing primarily on pre-set skill levels determined by outside authorities, we are sacrificing the very development of capacities that will shape our future and move us forward as a society. We are forfeiting future human capital in the test mills of today's classrooms.

Anyone who has ever worked in a classroom or has tried to understand child development knows that those who are closest to the children often have the best insights as to how to educate. Peggy Cooper, one of the participants in a Waldorf Teacher Education Program at Antioch New England summer sequence program for experienced educators has this to say:

> For me, the real heart of the process of research manifests itself in my everyday work with children. The in-depth reading can then find support to my on-going process as a teacher. Life is a constant state of becoming. When we do not work with the principle of continuous growth, we lose an important dynamic in our work with children, and we also run the risk of materialization of the spirit (dogmatizing something that should be an on-going process of maturation). Everyday is a

new opportunity to learn from our work. What I discovered in my independent study research is that data gathered from a living process is a vital and valid way to sustain continuous research as a teacher.

Good teaching is a responsive activity; watching and observing the activities and interests of children leads to innovative lesson plans and creative group activities. Dedicated teachers are tired of being told what to do by people who do not understand the spirit of childhood. It is time to begin a new chapter in education by fighting for the emancipation of the teacher.

2. BACK OFF, BIG BROTHER!

MORE THAN THREE decades ago, John Fentress Gardner spoke words that are more than ever relevant today:

> America today is dispirited. She is fast losing her vision and her confidence. She waits to be lifted. She longs to be renewed. But the only way for our country to open up a full draft of fresh inspiration is through coming closer again to spiritual insights and values! And this can be done for the nation as a whole only through education. But this opening up of the wellspring of what alone makes life worthwhile cannot be undertaken until a 'wall of separation' has been raised between *school* and state similar to the one the First Amendment raised long ago between *church* and state. All schools must become independent schools.[8]

I would like to begin by distinguishing between "independent" and "private." Because of early initiatives in higher education in North America such as William and Mary College, Harvard and others, the notion of private education took hold and was the exclusive domain of those who could afford such an education. Thanks to Horace Mann and others, public schools were eventually founded on the premise that education should be open to all. Without going into an extensive recapitulation of the history of American education, let us suffice to say that for over two hundred years we have had two strands, the one preserved as the Harvard legacy called private education and the other being our public schools. Even our university system has perpetuated this division into state universities and private colleges. Those included in the private sector are often more expensive and value selectivity, while those in the public realm value open access to all. These two currents run throughout our society, offering competing values of individuality vs. inclusion.

In my view, an "independent" school combines the values of both, in that such a school tries to serve "the public" by providing quality education to a diverse group of students while refusing to accept government mandates and testing requirements. An independent school is not necessarily made up of wealthy families, as most have active scholarship programs and enlist the parents in seeking broad community support through voluntary contributions. Most of all, independent schools value the insight of teachers in setting policy and the freedom of parents to select a school of their choice.

Thus in his call for all schools to become independent, John Gardner did not mean privatization but rather freeing schools from state and federal control. The closest things we have today in this regard are the increasingly popular charter schools which are granted permission to operate, often with considerable freedom. However, testing and teacher licensure remain an issue in many cases.

The notion that the government should guide education is deeply ingrained in the mindset of most people today. We turn to the state or federal government whenever we have a social challenge and it is hard to find a new way of working things out. In 1919, Rudolf Steiner, the Austrian scientist and educator who started the Waldorf School in Stuttgart that year, spoke on behalf of the freedom of the teacher:

> One can only do one's work as an educator when one stands in a free, individual relationship to the pupil one teaches. One must know that, for the guidelines of one's work, one is dependent only on *knowledge of human nature,* the principles of social life and such things, but not upon *regulations or laws* prescribed from the outside.... The growing human being should mature with the aid of educators and teachers independent of the state and economic system, educators who can allow individual faculties to develop freely because their own have been given free rein.[9]

In order for this to take place, Steiner advocated for the complete disassociation of the educational system from government and industry: "The place and function of educators within society should depend solely upon the authority of those engaged in this activity. The administration of the educational institutions, the organization of courses of instruction and their goals should be entirely in the hands of persons who themselves are *simultaneously* either teaching or otherwise productively engaged in cultural life."[10]

Briefly stated, Steiner envisioned a reordering of the social life that would include three distinct spheres

of activity, the "rights life" that is commonly understood as part of governance, the economic realm which
includes the production and distribution of goods and
services, and the cultural life. He felt that these areas
needed to be distinct even while interacting with one
another so as to allow the potential of each sphere of
activity to manifest unencumbered.

What is meant by "cultural life?" Here one can
include the Metropolitan Museum of Art in New York
City, the local children's museum, the regional music
or dance company, universities, schools and learning
centers—any grouping of people who are dedicated
to the development of human capacities. People in
these groups participate out of a common vision and
recognize talent in all forms. The key ingredient in
these cultural groups is the free unfolding of human
potential over time. The theatrical performance I
attended a few nights ago may continue to influence
me for days, even years to come. The value of what
those professionals offered cannot be measured by the
ticket price—in fact, the admission was actually just
my voluntary contribution to their work. They gave
me so much to discuss and remember. A good performance can nourish the soul. Indeed, many of these cultural institutions reach out to the community through
enrichment programs with the schools to encourage
attendance and participation.

The cultural sphere is distinct from the economic
realm, which is dedicated to the creation of goods
and services that support our human needs for living.
If one stops to examine the shoe one is wearing, it
quickly becomes apparent that many people, all over
the world contributed to the production, distribution

and sale of the shoe. In the economic realm we are inextricably bound up with our brothers and sisters all over the world. With the sphere of government which is meant primarily to promote the equal rights of all— no matter what status or degree one might hold—we each have the same essential right to clean water, fresh air, and basic governmental functions. Above all, we have the right to vote, and this ensures that each person is heard in regard to the common good. These three spheres—the cultural, economic and rights realm—all have a valid place in society.

The difficulty arises when one sphere infringes on another, thus stifling the human spirit. This happens, as mentioned earlier, when the government legislates standards for schools or micromanages business. But it also works the other way around; schools for profit, run by corporations, are likewise not a good idea, as education has a longer time line than the bottom line of a business. We do not see the true fruits of good teaching until someone is well into adulthood—or many years later. Finally, when business tries to infringe on governmental processes through lobbyists, special interests and expense-paid trips, healthy governance is subverted. We need to establish stronger firewalls between the three spheres, between cultural institutions, business, and government. Only then will the three best serve human interests.

Yet one may ask, if the government stays out of the conduct of schools, how can one ensure that there will be any standards, any level of accountability? Here we can borrow a page or two from our academic traditions in higher education. Just as there are accreditation agencies that help universities adhere to their espoused standards, so also we can establish cross-district accreditation agencies that would be staffed by current or former teachers. They would help monitor school progress and help independent schools establish long-range plans, set goals and find resources to achieve them. The point of this approach is that *the profession itself* would see to accountability, not the government. Thus when there are challenges one could turn to people who understand the dynamics of the classroom. Decisions might be made more on the basis of insight rather than politics.

Independence in the cultural realm of education will only survive the test of time if teachers engage in vigorous professional development. One of the best ways to do this is classroom-based, action research. In order to achieve and maintain high standards in education, we need to look more closely at the ways in which teachers can actively participate in classroom research that would then be subject to peer review. Janey Newton, who participated in the Waldorf Teacher Education Program at Antioch University, explains how this manifested for her:

> The activity of engaging ourselves in individual research projects brings a real liveliness to the study of Anthroposophy and Waldorf education. When a topic such as the wisdom of fairy tales is researched, put into practice, and shared among colleagues, it gains a strength that it didn't have before. The kernels of truth that have been lifted from the research on practical applications can be planted in other Waldorf classrooms and life situations. This idea of shared research is much

like re-seeding the garden each year so that it will continue to flourish.

In the following chapters I will demonstrate that responsible research can renew the curriculum, raise standards and enhance teacher learning without the imposition of external mandates and standards.

3. INTRODUCTION TO RESEARCH

TEACHERS THE WORLD over have questions about their work, about the children they teach, lessons, materials, and the functioning of schools as social organizations. These questions are real; they come from participation in the living stream of education. But are these questions given a chance to resound in the cacophony of demands on teachers today? How can we make space for true questions arising out of classroom practice?

In striving to meet the needs of children, teachers practice observation. They look at temperaments and learning styles, social interactions, handwriting, walking, speaking and drawing, among other things. These observations are often child specific, yet relate to the age group in general. Many of these observations provoke insights that can be helpful to other teachers. Can we find ways to share these child-centered observations beyond the faculty circle in one particular school?

Many teachers become librarians. They collect poems, songs, stories, skits, circle activities, science experiments, readers and plays until after some years a teacher may possess a veritable treasure trove of materials. Within a school, there is often considerable sharing. Yet much more could be done to share resources. Beyond the collection of materials there are the gems, those primary resources developed by teachers with special creativity and insight. I am speaking about original work, the creative stories, plays, activities and lessons that were created in a burst of enthusiasm in response to a particular challenge or classroom situation. How can we foster and expand this creativity?

By the very nature of their tasks, teachers follow a path of inquiry. Yet the focus often shifts from week to week and block to block depending upon immediate demands. There is a need to focus and organize our research efforts, now more than ever due to the mounting concerns with ever-increasing government regulation and standardized testing as pointed out previously. Bethany Craig from the Waldorf Teacher Education Program at Antioch concurs:

> Research is essential for the carpenter as well as for the teacher as well as for the philosopher. In order to work at the highest level possible, it is necessary to equip oneself with the best tools. But the question of research goes beyond the act of acquiring information. Life is a continual flow. In order to offer something, work, thoughts, whatever, to the world and to society, there must be an incoming flow to the doer and this is research whether of a factual or spiritual nature. It is food for humanity.

In order to begin working with some of the questions raised in the above paragraphs, the sections that follow will look at some of the obstacles common to classroom research, possible goals and methods, working with a question, and organizing and sharing. One section will describe a possible collaborative model for teacher research, and the conclusion will consider the spiritual implications of re-searching. This is not an exhaustive study on research. The aim is to stimulate inquiry, discussion and the practice of research in schools.

4. PERCEPTIONS OF OBSTACLES TO TEACHER RESEARCH

IN SPEAKING WITH practicing teachers, three constraints are repeated again and again: time, resources and support. Here are the voices of a few public school teachers considering research:

> *Time, time, time—resources, resources.... Can we look at teachers as professionals? As researchers? Should we look at teachers-researchers differently than teachers, and invoke incentives to do research...money, perhaps, but also time, recognition, space to try new ideas ... support?*

> *Teachers seem to need more free time for research and for renewal. I wish schools could recognize this and somehow provide periods of time for professional work...perhaps floating teachers would help.*

> *Consider the economic and political implications of such research. What (administrative) entities have a vested interest in squelching it?*

> *Time, support, recognition of teachers as professionals and as people with expertise.... The daily stress and demands right now are too much. We*

can't add more to teachers' lives. We must be able to incorporate research into present teaching.... Less would lead to more, more opportunities for meaningful research.

Please consider our current time and isolating constraints. How can we convince the wider voting communities and administrators that we need time and each other—for the benefit of the children?

Given the increase in mandated material, it is no wonder that so many of the above teacher comments focus on time. The nature of the challenge may vary depending on each school, but the general themes emerging from Waldorf and public school teachers are remarkably similar. Any effort to enhance teacher research will by necessity have to take full account of the obstacles they face.

But looking squarely at the challenges also provides an opportunity to re-conceive, re-design and re-think traditional assumptions about research. We need to reframe what we consider to be research—a point developed more fully in the next chapter—and start to see teacher research as an extension of learning and living. Over the years I have found that if I simply "adopt" a question or theme for a while, I start to collect materials, meet people, have ideas, and gradually a new project emerges. One need not take a year off from work to focus learning by way of qualitative research. However, any research effort by practicing teachers needs to begin with an understanding of the following points:

1. A teacher's primary task is to teach. Any research has to enhance teaching, if it is to be meaningful both to the teacher and the children.

2. It would be naïve to postulate that research does not consume a commodity in short supply, namely time. So rather than adding another layer of work onto the teacher s day, how can research actually enhance the quality of teaching and thus potentially save time in the end? If one can describe a situation in which preparation is facilitated and relationships within the school strengthened through research, one might be able to justify allocating some precious time for research. But for practicing teachers, the results need to be practical and viable if research is to be sustained over time.

3. Methods used in such research will need to be in harmony with the demands of classroom and the school day. Thus my main objective in the chapter on "methods" will be to demonstrate just how many possibilities are available for valuable research. One does not need to spend hours in the library to arrive at findings that may enhance education in more than one classroom.

4. If these findings are to have value beyond the life and the classroom of one particular teacher, we will need to find ways of sharing information that go beyond the traditional route of scholarly publication. Teacher research is meant to be used.

5. The above points translate into a bias towards qualitative research rather than traditional quantitative research.

Melissa McCall explains this point from her participation at Antioch:

> As I mulled over this question, I realized that, as an avid reader and quester, I've been engaged in a life long research project. Yet, in my work of delving into the wisdom of fairy tales this past year, I noticed a real shift in lifestyle. Though I only scratched the surface of this rich topic, the changes came in my whole attitude. "I'm doing research," I often found myself reporting proudly to anyone who would listen. Being in this mode meant that I was able to digest and articulate the material in a living way.
>
> Knowing that my Antioch group-mates were similarly engaged was a great source of strength during the intense research period. I intend to take up a new research project (on the Sophia) in September. I'm interested in hearing more about collaborative research.

As Glenda Bissex said when she gave a guest presentation during my course on educational research: "Quantitative research seeks to prove something; qualitative research seeks to learn something."

Teacher research is all about learning.[11]

5. REINVENTING RESEARCH: NEW CONCEPTS, NEW APPROACHES

A S AN EXPERIMENT, I asked a group of people to give me a string of words that comes to mind when hearing the term "research." They brainstormed as follows—library, footnotes, readings, communication, scary, deadlines, interviews, dry, stressful, graphs, bibliographies, hypothesizing, notes, data, variables, control groups, stilted—to name but a few. Needless to say, I was surprised to hear that most of these words described traditional approaches to research. No wonder teachers have found little time for such work.

If re-search means to look again and again, to be open to the unknown in the search for new meaning, then perhaps we need to begin with a new characterization of "research" itself. Traditional research, by the way, is not really that open to the unexpected, since the hypothesis anticipates an answer, and the data collected is supposed to be solid enough to constitute "proof." Yet if one does a survey of the history of scientific research, for instance, one quickly realizes how soon the conclusions of one year are submerged by the totally new discoveries of the next. Besides, in the case of teachers, proof is often less important than learning. As stated by David Hopkins, "Teachers and researchers do not conceptualize teaching the same way. They live in different intellectual worlds and so their meanings rarely connect...the usual form of educational research, the psycho-statistical or agricultural-botany paradigm, has severe limitations as a method of construing and making sense of classroom reality."[12] Thus teachers need a different approach to research if it is to have practical value.

In redefining "research" we can begin by illustrating our goals. For teachers, these might include:

1. Rather than serve as a means of gathering information, research for teachers can be a vehicle for gaining understanding.[13] This means formulating your own questions, selecting a method that works for your results, which may not change the world but might very well change an aspect of your own teaching. Research for understanding involves a search for meaning rather than proof.

2. Being prepared for the unexpected, which requires an open mind and heart and a willingness to be surprised. Rather than an emphasis on control, teacher research needs to be flexible and varied. We will discuss this further in the chapter on methods. As Ann Sauer states from her own experience through the Waldorf Teacher Education Program at Antioch, "The idea of doing educational research sounded somewhat dreadful until the actual midpoint of my first project. By then I had done enough reading, interviewing and observing that exciting correlations were

forming. Questions arose that I lived with as
I continued looking into the literature and
observing children. The actual paper writing
was a renewal and portal for future research. I
learned that research creates faculties we may
use for greater understanding of our children."
This example of direct experience along with
other observations convinces me that this
attitude of open-mindedness has spiritual and
pedagogical value in itself, even if nothing
else is "accomplished" in the research process.

3. These qualities of openness and flexibility
   do not negate the need for the discipline of
   inquiry. Once a question is identified and
   articulated, one goal is to follow its path with
   consistency and true discipleship. If it is one's
   own question that one is following, if one
   owns it, the systematic line of inquiry will be
   less onerous.

4. This leads to another goal: teacher research
   must be driven by burning interest. If one is
   not interested enough in a question to live
   with it for many months, find another one. The
   initial question needs an element of passion in
   order to be a long-term companion.

5. Since teachers spend most of their time in
   action, doing things in the classroom with
   children, teacher-driven research needs to
   be action based. "Put simply, action research
   is the way groups of people organize the
   conditions under which they can learn from
   their own experience."[14] Action research
   can involve four phases: planning, acting,

observing and reflecting. Much of this can be done in the classroom while teaching.

6. A final goal of teaching research involves the word commitment. Oh, how much is perpetrated in the name of this word. Yet, if research is to take hold in our schools, we need teachers who are committed to a path of inquiry. Given the constraints on time and energy, I suggest a research commitment to a small question, something that might seem insignificant at first. For instance, rather than take a theme such as "How do children respond to mathematics when taught through movement in grades 1 to 5?" the teacher might begin with something that has clear parameters: "Are children more attentive on Monday mornings if the day begins with math-movement activities?" Make a commitment to something that can be completed. Above all, make sure that the question selected directly relates to the rest of your teaching life. Judith Selin's experience at Antioch illustrates this point well: "To devote time that allows immersion into research is a gift to oneself. It is also a beginning in many ways. To begin with the whole of the universe and its mysteries, to take one idea from it, to develop and explore it, to find its connections to the whole—in this, we find understanding, growth and confidence. We feel more empowered by our understanding and realize that this can be a beginning, a way for us to see the world one piece at a time."

6. WHY DO RESEARCH?

IN THE SPRING 1994 issue of *Teacher Research*, Karen Ernest describes her experiences creating a community of learning, a group of teacher researchers. Afterwards, she asked the teachers to review their work together. The participants felt that the project had affected their classroom work in the following ways: "Increased sense of professionalism; increased support for their own work through participation in a community of colleagues; support for changes in what or how they teach; awareness and practice in observation and reflection on their classroom; sense of empowerment to answer questions, challenge the status quo; and suggestions for change in teaching practice."[15]

This summary statement prompts a more detailed examination of the benefits of teacher research and why this activity should be pursued more vigorously. What follows are some of the most frequently cited reasons based on the literature I have reviewed.

THE PERFORMANCE GAP

A growing body of research suggests, first, that there is often incongruence between a teacher's publicly declared philosophy of beliefs about education and how he or she behaves in the classroom. Second, there is often incongruence between the teacher's declared goals and objectives and the way in which the lesson is actually taught. Third, there is often a discrepancy between a teacher's perceptions or account of a lesson and the perceptions or account of other participants (e.g. pupils or observers) in the classroom (Vide, Elbaz 1983). All of these discrepancies reflect a gap between behavior and intention and are a source for classroom research problems.[16]

Thus this gap between what is and what could be becomes a rationale for collaborative research. One might say that the kind of research model proposed at the end of this pamphlet, a regional linkage of schools around research conferences, could help keep us honest. Research is a means of self-evaluation and professional feedback.

PROFESSIONAL DEVELOPMENT

It follows that teacher-directed research is likely to enhance teaching practices as the participant engages in a process of questioning, observing, refining, and reshaping attitudes and opinions. This process of personal growth and change can have a liberating effect on the profession as a whole. In recent years, state governments have imposed a web of restrictions and controls on public schools and have occasionally even ventured into the domain of private education. The public in general seems to continually demand more accountability from teachers and clearly defined educational "outcomes." How can teachers respond to these demands? One way is to emphasize more internal accountability, to establish standards and goals based on teacher-driven research findings, and not those of local politicians, thereby reclaiming freedom in culture and education. "By adopting a research stance, teachers are liberating themselves from the control position they so often find themselves in."[17]

Increased public scrutiny can thus become an opportunity to emphasize professionalism rather than arbitrary criteria such as the norms set by standardized tests and Goals 2000. Teachers can assert leadership in their profession by shouldering more responsibility for their actions and creating a dynamic, creative learning environment through research.

TEACHERS AS ROLE MODELS

Children learn not only through what is presented but also by how the teacher goes about his or her own process of learning. Someone who is eagerly pursuing a theme in research will provide a role model for the children even if the subject itself is not shared in the classroom. Teacher research feeds the children; for, as described at the end of this book, when a teacher's ego intensifies its work on the lower members, this transformative activity can enhance the quality of all teacher/child interactions. Thus, rather than being a cold, cerebral activity, research can actually increase the intimacy of relationships.

SHARED VALUES

In the citation that began this section, the teachers used the word "support" several times in a few lines. Usually one thinks of research as a lonely activity, something that might only increase a sense of alienation and separation from the rest of the world as one sits in the local library. Yet an action-research model could become just the opposite. If one works as a team within the faculty, engages in classroom research with the students as collaborators, and shares the results with colleagues on a regular basis, one can accentuate the school as a community of learners with shared goals. This process can be sustaining and deeply encouraging.

OBSERVATION

The following story told by Michael Patton illustrates the power of observation when one is open to what the world has to teach, as well as the inductive analysis to extract meaning from simple phenomena that may have escaped the attention of other people:

> The story of the invention of modern running shoes illustrates these principles. The design of sneakers varied little until the 1960s, when competitive runners began to turn to lighter-weight shoes. Reducing the weight of shoes clearly improved performance, but problems of traction remained. A running coach, Bill Bowerman, went into the sneaker business in 1962. He paid close attention to the interest in lighter-weight shoes and the problems of traction. One morning while he was making waffles he had an idea. He heated a piece of rubber in the waffle iron to produce the first waffle-shaped sole pattern that became the world standard for running shoes. Subsequently engineers and computers would be used to design and test the best waffle patterns—but the

initial discovery came from paying close attention, being open, making connections, drawing
on personal experience, getting a feel for what
was possible, exploration, documenting initial
results, and applying what he had learned.[18]

As long as we focus only on what we expect to
see, we are functionally blind. To quote Glenda Bis-
sez again, "The world around us is a text, and we have
stopped being able to read much of it. We listen to
the weather report rather than looking at the sky."[19]
Research can bring us out of the realm of weather
reports and connect us with the sky, the primordial
expanse of real learning through observation. All
teachers rely on secondary materials, source books,
curriculum guides, lessons from other teachers, but
do we have enough primary sources? It would be very
healthy for our schools as cultural institutions if we
once dared to throw out all the accumulated materials
from other people and had to teach from direct observation of our students' needs. Any research question
based on classroom/school life, no matter how limited
in scope, has the potential of sharpening our skills
in observation that could then apply to a wide range
of other activities. For example, observing how the
children learn on Monday mornings before and after
gross motor movement activities would heighten the
teacher's awareness of student responses throughout
the week. Teacher research is needed not only for the
specific findings that may arise, but also for the all-
important by-products, such as a change in teacher
consciousness. Once one really observes, one cannot
stop. Research through observation becomes a healthy
habit.

As a side remark, I would like to draw a small yet vital distinction between observation and inference. As Ted Sizer states in *Horace's Compromise*, "Everyday experiences show how important this distinction is. SAT scores have gone up two points. Some then hypothesize that because SAT scores have gone up, high schools must be getting tougher. The first statement is an observation, and the second a conclusion (of substantial dubiousness) drawn from the observation. Sloppy people confuse the two."[20]

Social Change

Any meaningful teacher research has the potential to effect social change. One has only to read Paulo Freire's *Pedagogy of the Oppressed* to experience a vivid, anguished example of how educational emancipation goes hand in hand with social and political change. I can imagine a path of social/political emancipation as follows:

Teacher research as intense professional/spiritual striving can lead to

An enhanced professional "voice" for teachers, which can lead to

Strong, vibrant schools that serve as cultural centers, which can lead to

Freedom for education and necessary restrictions on political and economic intrusions on cultural endeavors in general, which may result in a reconfiguration of the social organism.

Barbara Bedingfield's comments on her participation in the Waldorf Teacher Education Program at Antioch New England are a clear example. "My independent research which centered on the topic of child observation helped me to deepen my understanding of the child as she unfolds during each developmental stage and to look with *new* eyes in a comprehensive way at every child. Knowledge led to interest and interest to love, a love, I trust, that will guide me in my work with children." So if one considers the above points valid reasons for engaging and supporting classroom research, one then has to start looking at the beginning of the process, finding the questions or focus of study.

7. SEEING, FEELING, FINDING YOUR QUESTION

W E ALL ASK questions, of others, and ourselves all the time. These questions are varied and often not even verbalized. Some of our questions are factual in nature and are answered immediately: "Do I turn left on Hickory Street? How much does this watermelon cost?" Other questions stay with us for a while: "How come, whenever I sit down to do some work at my desk, the phone always rings?" There are also questions that become companions, questions that remain with us for an extended period of time. It is these that are the focus of discussion in this section.

Traditional research suggests that you begin with a problem. If this is hard to identify, you might start a few sentences with the following phrases:

> I would like to improve the ...
> Some people are unhappy about ...
> What can I do to change the situation ...?
> I am perplexed by ... [21]

My preference is to find a question rather than a problem and to do a series of "wonderings"—I wonder how.... I wonder about... I wonder if.... To identify yours you might make a long list in a stream of consciousness manner, then go back and find groupings, those that involve your class, the material, relationships, etc. When you have found your family of questions, try and formulate one question that speaks to the core issue.

Then try out your question on others. When I recently taught a workshop on educational research in Ann Arbor, Michigan, I asked participants to write their question at the top of a blank page and pass it to the person on the left. We each had to react to the question in front of us. Some of the responses to the questions from those who received them were along these lines: What do you really mean? This is not clear. Alternative phrasing could be: Have you considered...? This is really three issues.... You might call so and so ... and so on. Then we passed the pages to the next person, and so our questions made the rounds, receiving in all twenty-two responses. When our own questions had been returned to us after this "round robin" exercise, I asked that the feedback be considered overnight before we had small-group meetings and individuals wrote up formal proposals for research. Most of the students in the class felt that this exercise was extremely helpful in terms of clarifying their thinking and that it also served as a validation of their issue and personal needs.

It is also possible to begin the research process without a clearly defined question. Here is another pearl from Glenda Bissex: "One thing that I've learned from myself as an observer is how I can unearth or excavate my own questions by following my own observations. What attracts my attention as I observe and what I find myself recording is information to help me answer questions that I may not yet have consciously asked."[22]

Thus the process of finding a question and learning from it is a spiritual process that will be considered again in the last section of this book.

Jon Wagner, author of *Ignorance in Educational Research* speaks of how research can be designed to fill in "blank spots" in terms of questions already formulated and when one simply needs more information, or how research can provoke new questions that illuminate "blind spots" in existing theories, methods and perceptions.[23] Both avenues help us see the phenomena before us more clearly than before.

Harry Wolcott, another resource for the teacher-researcher, is attracted to the idea "of thinking about research as problem setting, rather than problem solving."[24] This consideration is helpful because teacher-researchers might inadvertently set themselves up for failure if they expect to solve all their "problems" through research. It is important to remember that success and failure can only be judged in relation to what you set out to do. Therefore don't bite off more than you can chew. Finding questions, formulating problems and key issues is in itself a worthy result of research. As with the Grail Mystery and the story of Parcifal, the educator might be content to plead: May I be so *present* that, if nothing else, I learn to ask the right questions.

Finally this quote from Sandra Ruggiero, a participant in the Waldorf Teacher Education Program at Antioch, shows us one result that an open approach to research can have. "Doing research gives one an opportunity to delve into something with a depth that life seldom allows for in this day and age. It can be a counterpoint to balance the alacrity and shallowness of our other daily demands and pressures. To carry a question into waking and sleeping and through trans-formations of your own thinking is almost a form of meditation. To write it down is to allow others to also drink from the deep waters of your refreshing pool."

This does not rule out the possibility for more tra-ditional research if a teacher is so inclined. (See the appendix for a chart of different types of research.) The above paragraphs describe a more open system in which the teacher engages in an activity that provides an issue and the basis for action research. Yet if one wishes to follow a more closed system, one can also formulate a hypothesis and engage in research that will supply data to support the theory. With this latter approach, and indeed with all research, it is particu-larly important to find the appropriate methods.

8. THOUGHTS ON RESEARCH METHODS

BEFORE DELVING INTO specific suggestions on methodology, I would like to share a few reflections in a general way. The most significant discovery I made in my own research efforts was that much can be discovered by using what is already at hand. One does not need to get on a plane, send away for all sorts of material, or run up a long phone bill in doing research. It is best to start with whatever happens to be readily available: the classroom, colleagues, parents, the students' work, and an ERIC search at the local library. By typing in a few key words one gets a deluge of articles and citations for any given topic, not to mention what happens by just Googling. It is possible that one might even save that plane ticket for the "last round" of the research, when one is thoroughly familiar with the subject and can make the best use of an exotic visit. To modify a popular bumper sticker, *research locally, think globally.*

Also, it is important to sound another theme at this early stage: consider those who are being researched. It is part of the abstract, (some might say) masculine tradition in research to delve in, collect the data one wants, and not consider the process from the point of view of those who are being observed. I suggest that, at each stage and with each method, consider "how it feels" from the other end, trying whenever possible to use nonintrusive methods of data collection. For example, instead of bringing in a video camera to observe social interactions (especially intrusive in a Waldorf classroom), try looking at carpet wear, listening to the children's comments, even examining the trash basket at the end of the day. Moreover, in an interview, it is not just the teacher who will be learning. Prepare a few questions, but leave time for those that may arise from the person being interviewed. The interview could also be considered a conversation. As one advisor in my doctoral program said, leave room for the unexpected in the interview conversation. (See the appendix for interviews and types of research.) Moreover, record your contributions in the discussion, because you may say something in the context of the interview to a particular person that would not have been possible if you had stuck to a straight question/answer format. In other words, you might discover something through the act of speaking.

Finally, by way of introductory comments, use triangulation. The suspicion concerning qualitative research has often been that it will be "soft" and unreliable. This makes triangulation all the more significant in terms of your credibility. Briefly put, triangulation means using three or more means to answer the same question. Thus if you want to find out what children have for breakfast,

1. Ask them
2. Interview their parents
3. Send home a questionnaire to be completed over five days
4. At a class night, ask the parents to go over the results with you

The fourth step is one of my favorites. It again takes research out of the "superior, Ph.D. realm" and makes it a community event. You do not really know all the facts, yet after collecting some data, you are open to reviewing it with those who gave their time to help you. It also serves as a convenient way to correct misimpressions and possible bias on the part of the researcher. In real life, research is not a matter of data entry, but really a "spiraling in" toward greater understanding. Take your participants along on the journey.

What follows is not a list of methods to use, but rather an array of possibilities. Some may be more suitable for one given project than another. The element of freedom arises when one overcomes one's natural inclinations and tries a variety of techniques.

1) **Be Awake in the Moment**. As stated above, use the classroom. Examine your daily routine, the lesson and the human interactions in the light of your question. There is much that can be found in the ordinary.

2) **Field Notes**. Buy yourself a new binder with loose-leaf pages. Keep it on your desk in the classroom. In the morning, before the children arrive, reformulate your question at the top of the page, and enter the date. Then, during the day, make short entries; incomplete sentences are fine for this exercise. At the end of the day, make additions that were not possible while in the middle of things. Use descriptions, and do not worry if things do not agree with each other. This method of taking field notes helps focus you on the issue over a period of time, and is good for general impressions and descriptions that can later be interpreted.

3) **Audio Tape Recording**. Most Waldorf teachers discourage use of electronic devices, and for good reason. Yet there are ways to work with tape recording that I have found invaluable and should at least be considered in certain circumstances. A small tape recorder (I have one the size of my appointment book) can be kept in a desk drawer, or between two books. It can be turned on without any noise, used for brief periods, and then erased after listening to it in the evening. It is particularly useful for one-on-one interactions, less helpful when there is a lot of background classroom activity. If nothing else, a tape, done occasionally, can supplement other methods and help us listen with greater accuracy.

4) **Video Tape Recording**. This method is used increasingly in public schools and even in traditional teacher education programs. It is certainly intrusive, and I would not use it with young children. (The same is true with some of the constant use of cameras at some of our assemblies and class plays.) Yet if working with older students, colleagues, parents or a community event, this method might be helpful in one's research, as one can view the interview or interaction again and again. Also, when one sees oneself in the video, it can promote a re-examination of gesture, movement and interpersonal interactions.

5) **Pupil Diaries**. In many schools students are asked to keep a journal or daily log at one grade level or another. This practice can double for teacher research, in that your assignment to them might include an aspect that you are investigating. Since you will be checking their work anyway, this method of teacher research is highly time-efficient. Likewise, the student

journal entries provide a stimulating counterpart to one's own fieldwork (#2 above).

6) **Questionnaires**. More appropriate for older students and adults, this method allows you to ask very specific questions of a large number of people. Someone other than you can collate the information if you are pressed for time, especially if you have used a scale such as "often, seldom, never." For open-ended questions, I suggest you read each one yourself, for often things are said "between the lines." One tip—do a trial run first and then rewrite your questions. It is amazing how many ways a simple question can be understood. You want feedback from a few people so as to make your mistakes on a small scale before distributing the questionnaire to the masses. Also, it is not just the responses to specific questions that are of interest to the researcher, but the correlation of responses. You might even formulate the same question in different ways at various points in the survey.

A questionnaire allows you to cast a broad net and involve many people in your work. I advise my Antioch students to use this method early on in a research project, as it also helps to identify issues and people for subsequent stages.

7) **Case Studies**. "A case study is individual research in a small context. We don't know enough based on our individual classroom case studies to know which are the generalizations that will hold true for other teachers. But other teachers will know. As teacher researchers, we can't make those generalizations, but they will be made by our readers. I believe our classroom case studies can offer valuable insights for other teachers, but the basis for those insights is

not generalizations, but universals, which is also what makes literature endure. The things we have in common as human beings—those fundamental things that we have in common as teachers—are going to be there, in those case studies or pieces of literature. They endure because they continue to speak to what is fundamental in human experience, or in teaching experience."[25]

I found in my research that case studies were like writing a biography. I really got to know the people I worked with. After using some of the above-mentioned methods, it was also refreshing to go into depth and explore issues with someone over time. We especially need more longitudinal studies of children as they progress through the grades. The case study informs and compliments the material gathered by other means.

8) **Documentary Evidence**. This sounds like the work of a detective, but it is actually one of the most readily available methods for Waldorf teachers. Our students create a wealth of material: main lesson books, compositions, drawings, paintings, homework assignments and projects. All this becomes fodder for the researcher, if the eye is trained to observe. This means not just living in the moment with the child as the work is created, but afterwards stepping back and *seeing it again* with the eye of a researcher.

If nothing else, write your research question in big letters and stand it up on your desk. Then take a pile of the children's creations and look at each one in light of your inquiry. You will be amazed at what can be found.

9) **Peer Observation**. We often do not visit each other's classrooms enough. One way to build community in the school, share resources and do research is to schedule a series of peer visits. Give your visitor a 5x8 note card with your questions or issues, and ask him or her to observe your lesson with these in mind. Be sure to have the follow-up conversation. Much may have been observed that you missed. Take notes during the dialogue. Write them up and a few days later share them with the colleague who visited. Again, this kind of research method helps create a circle of care.

10) **Critical Incidence Research**. We all know about those unexpected "happenings" that occur from time to time in schools. Use them. If an incident occurs on the playground between two children, observe and record exactly what transpires as it may in fact speak to larger issues that live in the social fabric of the class. Or take a series of incidents in one class over time and look at them. How did you respond? What was revealed? The critical incident is like a moment of wakefulness that can shed light on the larger picture.

11) **Interviews**. Already mentioned above, I would simply like to add that one needs to be aware of the types of questions one asks (see appendix). For instance, certain kinds of questions will prompt dichotomous responses such as Yes, No, Yeah, Sort of, and so on. Open-ended questions tend to draw a person out. Sometimes one might even want to ask questions that have a lead-in or presupposition such as: How effective do you think the foreign language program is at this school? Here you are presupposing that the person interviewed can make a judgment

about the program. Clarity of intent on your part is essential if the interviews are to be successful. Know the difference between what, how, when and why questions.

In addition to the usual type of interviews you might conduct, there are third-party interviews that you may not have considered: classroom observer/student, student/student, and observer/observer. You can facilitate the gathering of data without always being at the center of the action.

12) **Other methods** might include sociometry, slide/tape photography, clinical supervision, highly structured observation by an outsider, checklists, coding scales and much more. The best methods often arise when you are frustrated in using someone else's methods and you have to invent your own. Just be sure that you can clearly articulate what you are doing, and keep accurate records.

Educational research should include a literature review. What has been published on your theme? My students at Antioch have found the ERIC search in the computer lab invaluable. Even if you only scan much of the material, you need to know what others have done.

Finally, I need to say a few words about "human subjects testing." Each professional field has its own guidelines, and it is *essential* that researchers follow these guidelines. Any intervention that can affect the subjects being investigated must be scrutinized from this perspective. For instance, when I did my case studies, I asked the teachers involved to sign a consent form. Among other things, I promised not to release the information gathered to employers, to omit names if quotes are used, and in general, to do everything possible to respect the rights of those participating. In school situations, one may have to obtain parental consent for certain kinds of research. It is best to consult these professional guidelines *ahead of time.*

For those who want to read a much more comprehensive study of qualitative research, I suggest *Qualitative Evaluation and Research Methods* by Michael Quinn Patton. (Some of his charts appear in more detail in the appendix.) One can also consult teacher journals and go online to read about research conferences and presentations.

9. ORGANIZING A RESEARCH PROJECT

PICTURE YOURSELF BEING outrageously successful at all of the work discussed so far. Now you have a burning question (or two), lots of material has been collected through the use of documents, interviews, observations, case studies, and so on, and everything is heaped up on your table at home in one fascinating, but chaotic pile. There are many, when faced with this spectacle, who abandon the whole process at this point. Indeed, for the natural "pack rats" in our midst, it is far easier to amass a fortune than to organize, let alone analyze, the material. Yet, it is essential for the research process that one goes beyond collection to comprehension. Organizing the material involves considered synthesis before one can start on analysis.

I suggest you begin by outlining some broad categories within your theme. Separate your material accordingly. You may well change your categories after a while, but in the initial sorting you are also beginning to "mix and match" information that will create new insights. Be sure to go through all the data.

Now you arrive at the weeding phase. Harry Wolcott describes this well:

> The critical task in qualitative research is not to accumulate all the data you can, but to "can" (i.e.

get rid of) most of the data you accumulate. This requires constant winnowing. The trick is to discover essences and then to reveal them within sufficient context, without being mired by trying to include everything that could be described. Audio tapes, videotapes, and now computer capabilities entreat us to do just the opposite; they have gargantuan appetites and stomachs. Because we can accommodate ever-increasing quantities of data—mountains of it—we have to be careful not to get buried by avalanches of our own making.[26]

And, of course, the ready availability of copy machines and instant downloading has not helped simplify our lives.

In organizing, as with preparation for teaching, it is not how much material you have, but rather how well you have worked it through. This sifting and sorting helps to connect you with the essentials.

A few practical suggestions:

1. Use index cards or computer files, with the title of a category at the top of each section. You can move the cards or files around as need arises, but having the headings in front of you will keep things organized.

2. In terms of facts, figures and especially citations, get them right the first time. As I found when editing *School as a Journey*, one inaccurate or missing page number in the footnotes can take hours to rectify. Keep accurate records.

3. If you are going to write up your findings, decide early on if you will use the *Chicago Manual of Style* for your field or the APA standards. This can save a lot of time later on.

4. Keep a pencil and small notebook on you at all times. Even after the formal gathering of data is over (actually, it is never over, you just have to decide when to stop), you can have sudden inspirations or ideas that need to be noted down. Take advantage of the higher levels of cognition described in the last chapter—they are the gifts of the gods. Even long meetings are remarkably productive in birthing inspirational thoughts. Keep your notebook by your side.

As you are sorting things out, it helps to know what your general intent might be:

Are you doing basic research in a general way so as to contribute to the fundamental knowledge available on a given subject?

Are you doing *applied research* to illuminate a societal concern?

Or might you engage in *summative evaluation* to determine the effectiveness of a particular program?

On the other hand, you might intend to perform a *formative evaluation* to actually help improve a program.

Are you doing *action research* to solve a specific problem?[27]

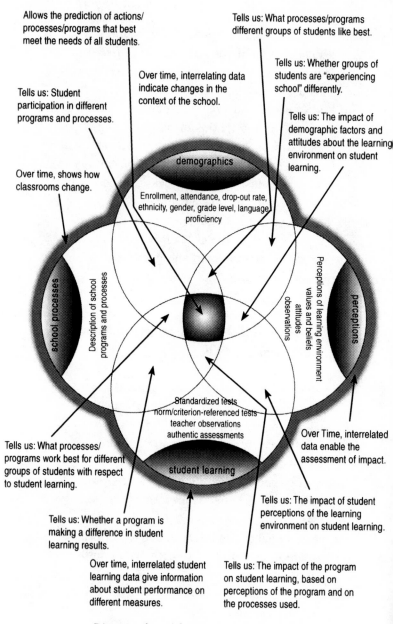

Allows the prediction of actions/processes/programs that best meet the needs of all students.

Tells us: What processes/programs different groups of students like best.

Over time, interrelating data indicate changes in the context of the school.

Tells us: Whether groups of students are "experiencing school" differently.

Tells us: Student participation in different programs and processes.

Tells us: The impact of demographic factors and attitudes about the learning environment on student learning.

Over time, shows how classrooms change.

demographics

Enrollment, attendance, drop-out rate, ethnicity, gender, grade level, language proficiency

school processes

Description of school programs and processes

Perceptions of learning environment values and beliefs attitudes observations

perceptions

Standardized tests norm/criterion-referenced tests teacher observations authentic assessments

student learning

Tells us: What processes/programs work best for different groups of students with respect to student learning.

Over Time, interrelated data enable the assessment of impact.

Tells us: Whether a program is making a difference in student learning results.

Tells us: The impact of student perceptions of the learning environment on student learning.

Over time, interrelated student learning data give information about student performance on different measures.

Tells us: The impact of the program on student learning, based on perceptions of the program and on the processes used.

Diagram adapted from Victoria L. Bernhardt, *Data Analysis for Comprehensive Schoolwide Improvement.*

Intentions give shape and form to material one gathers and organizes.

Then, when one has a good handle on *what* is available and *why* one is doing this work, it is time to start the analysis of the data. I find, at least in the student research that I review, that this aspect is usually the weakest, partly because it is given the least time, and partly because real analysis is strenuous and challenging. Most people are good at summarizing, but that is not analysis. Over the years I have had to be much more specific in coaching research projects by asking questions that provoke analysis: How do these findings compare with other studies? Are there contradictions between your work and that of others? How can you relate one subtopic in your project to another? What happens when you combine the results of your survey with the interview transcripts? How does this research relate to your own experience? How do things interact with one another, such as in the chart opposite, and how do the perceptions of school values and beliefs interact with student learning?

One has to move things around, draw diagrams, look at things from a variety of perspectives, and then one starts to do real analysis.

Collecting material is like going shopping, which is easy for most. Organizing and synthesizing the material is more challenging, much like preparing a meal. But the most complicated process of all, if one really stops to consider it, is the eating/digesting of the food. Research without analysis is like swallowing food without chewing properly. Good research values all stages of the process, including the nourishment and sharing that occurs when the food of learning is put to use. Marc Harrington gives us a succinct picture of this process based on his experience as a participant in the Waldorf Teacher Education Program at Antioch:

> I had no idea how much I was to learn doing this research! What began as an idea to incorporate the travel experience (somehow) into the learning environment of the Waldorf highschool student eventually turned into a study of [evil] forces at work in ancient Mayan ritual! And I got to bring twelve Waldorf highschool students to the ancient sites in the Yucatan (for a two-week trip) to boot! You never know where [the process of] research will lead you. A *tiny idea* can turn into a *career.* We ask questions that only we could ask. We investigate because it has become so much a part of what we find we need to know.

In our teaching, we can take what we've learned, of course, and apply it in the classroom. But just as important—through our striving to understand our subject (via research)—we naturally reflect this striving to our children, giving them a quiet example to which they can aspire.

10. Sharing Research

I F THE KIND of action research described in the foregoing pages is to have legitimacy within the larger circles of our profession, it needs to be shared. This not only means the articulation of what we have discovered, but the feedback and consequent corrective measures that are needed.

Although we may never feel we know enough on a given subject to share the results of our research, we do know something, and even that needs the enhancement of feedback. Sharing puts one in a vulnerable position; there are risks involved. Yet the social and intellectual benefits are great. One basic way to begin is to write.

In a marvelous article that appeared in *Handbook of Qualitative Research*, Laurel Richardson states, "I consider writing as a method of inquiry, a way of finding out about yourself and your topic ... Writing is also a way of "knowing"—a method of discovery and analysis. By writing in different ways, we discover new aspects of our topic and our relationship to it."[28] Thus writing is continued research, only on a different level. You are able to enter the imaginative realm as you become the creator of images.

I suggest you begin with a one-paragraph statement of purpose. If you cannot say the gist of your piece in one terse paragraph, it will certainly be harder to write a book. A statement of purpose can be as simple as the articulation of the issue or question studied, why you took it up, and the results. Remember in this whole endeavor, you are not trying to prove or define anything. Just describe and characterize and you will bring people along with you.

A characterization looks at things from several angles, keeps the image alive, focuses on the qualities, and does not try and define. Sometimes I advise students to pick up the phone and call a good friend. When the inevitable question arises, "So, what have you been doing lately," just turn on a tape recorder and say something about your research, why you took it up and the bottom line—the findings. Then after the rest of the phone conversation is over, replay the section on your research and write it down. It will need some editing, but most likely you have the gist of a statement of purpose.

My emphasis on this first stage comes from experience in reading student research reports and masters-level projects. If the first part, the purpose, is not in focus, everything else becomes much more difficult. There is a special kind of "soul economy" in spending the time chiseling a clear statement describing what the project is all about.

Then it is a natural next step to do an outline or sequence. Again, if past experiences with this sort of thing are intimidating, think of it as a table of contents. What are the main topics? In what order should they appear? Think about ways in which you can connect people with your work. What would interest your colleagues, your student's parents?

A solid outline can mark the start of some serious writing. However, in my experience, things have never been as linear as they seem on this page. I have found myself writing snippets even as the research progressed, and therefore the actual outline changes as one releases the creative stream of the narrative. The basic elements described here are important, but the actual experience, at least for me, is of unexpected simultaneity.

Along with "math phobia," "writer's block" ranks high on many people's most dreaded list. In large part, this is because writing is placed on such a high pedestal. It seems that many people subconsciously feel that if their work is not a bestseller they have failed as writers. Here you need to remember the above-cited words from Laurel Richardson. If writing is part of the process of discovery, you might lower your sights, practice some humility, and just aim to understand the material collected in a new way. Start the writing as a *reflection* on your findings. Begin in a conversational manner, just talking about your research. Use the pen or computer to do the talking. Don't worry about paragraphs or anything remotely close to proper grammar. Just say something about your work.

Harry Wolcott adds, "Writing is a form of thinking. Writers who indulge themselves by waiting until their thoughts are 'clear' run the risk of never starting at all."[29] Put something down on your screen or paper. If you are using word processing, it is easy to make deletions, cut and paste, and correct mistakes. Before the computer, doctoral candidates took twice as long to complete their studies.

In addition to technical assistance, the process of writing is enhanced by a certain amount of self-knowledge. Are you a morning or evening person? Do you need a stiff cup of coffee to get going, or a brisk walk? Know what works for you, and use it. For me, the early morning is writing time. Beginning in early May, I used to rise early each day and do one narrative, class-teacher report. After school was out, it was just a matter of making corrections and copying—a sufficiently onerous project in those warm June days.

Another suggestion: Consider the point at which you will quit each session and how to take up the writing again later. Instead of stopping at the end of a topic or section, I often find it best to stop just before the logical resting place or end of a chapter. This means that, at the next session, I was forced to reread the previous section, do some editing, and then jump back into the stream of things without having to pull everything up from scratch. Again, the important thing is knowing what works for you.

Another statement of the obvious: the shorter the piece, the more likely the possibility it will find readers. Qualitative research is meant to be read and used. If you can say it in a few words, do so.

Finally, at some point in the write-up you will need to inform the readers about the nature and extent of your database, how you collected the material and the methods used. They need to know how you went about your work, since the process influences the results. Again, when I read student reports, I usually turn first to the annotated bibliography. That tells me about process and enlightens my reading of the text.

These teacher research projects can be used for presentation in staff meetings, at a school board discussion of a particular topic, or as a brief piece in a local newspaper. Teachers can hold mini conferences to share their work, and schools could list completed projects in newsletters that go to parents. We have to be willing to make our work in education more visible. Remember—silence is complicity.

In 1992, the Waldorf Teacher Education Program at Antioch New England launched a summer sequence program for experienced educators. From the beginning, research was an integral part of the first year, as the students selected a theme to work with between the first and second summer sessions. After a year of "living with a question" and doing research as described in this book, they returned the following summer to take further courses and share their findings. I asked them to share reflections on the research process, some of which are included here and throughout this book.

The research and deepening of one's work, in my case foreign language teaching, can ignite renewed forces from within which can manifest themselves as enthusiasm and interest in one's teaching and working with the children. Through a deeper esoteric understanding and research in one's field and as an anthroposophist, the knowledge gained through research brings one closer together with fellow Waldorf teachers in a common striving. In this way, we can support each other and nurture each other through sharing of our work and findings.

(Sandra Houston)

Researching my topic was an opportunity to step back and understand the context the Waldorf schools occupy with regards to public education. By characterizing the public school approach to environmental education and science, I was able to go on to survey just what had been founded as an approach to nature in the Waldorf Schools. The most important aspect of the research was the new insights, which I was able to synthesize and develop from the wide range of literature, which I surveyed. My ability to speak intelligently about the Waldorf approach has greatly improved, and I believe my opinions are authentically grounded now in my own efforts and understanding. I would recommend research as a discipline to anyone who would wish to usher Waldorf education into the next century.

(Gregory Albright)

My anthroposophical research has a three-fold quality to it: the reading, the writing and the presentation. I found the quiet inner activity of research complemented the busy outer activity of my days. Reading with a question, a focus, increased my depth and encouraged me to wrestle with the material. This had a vivifying effect on my life. The process of writing went beyond compilation: it was as if all that I had taken in nurtured a seed within me. In tending this seed, it gradually ripened until something new had grown in me. Writing out of this inner conclusion was exhilarating. I then entered the social realm with the presentation of the essence of my work. This inspired me to take my paper to a different level, an imaginative "audience friendly" one, which led me to new insights on my topic. I breathed in with the research and out with the presentation. The whole process greatly strengthened me physically, emotionally and mentally. I have a solid footing in one aspect of Anthroposophy now and a matrix to which I can relate new information and insights. The spiral continues. The fruits multiply.

(Kathleen Reagan)

Winter evenings reading and carrying images into sleep; trips to the library, telephone conversations, stints at the computer—beginning to write things down. Searching, looking and finding again. Research? Gathering scattered threads together, starting to weave. Just a small piece of cloth, but so satisfying! Fit one small piece to another small piece, the cloth grows. This work made a rich and private inner haven for me—the task of writing, bringing my thoughts and feelings to form; seeing the rich colors swirl into shape and solidify. This was both a discovery and an exercise of will. Finally, presenting my winterwork to a group of colleagues spread the whole cloth out, a blanket for our mental picnic. I experienced this task as a way of connecting—with myself, with others and with the world that holds us all.

(Kate Gage)

11. A COLLABORATIVE MODEL FOR TEACHER RESEARCH

LOOKING AT THE larger picture of teacher stress and renewal, as I did during my doctoral research, I found that caregivers—nurses, parents, and teachers—also need nurturing. To give without replenishment is to limit one's capacity to continue. How can one find the resources for personal and professional renewal?

I found that many teachers, despite participating in numerous meetings, often felt a high degree of isolation. Not only do our tasks limit the time we can converse together on a personal level, but the level of expectations are such that many feel inadequate, whether it be in drawing, singing, math or speech. It is hard to reach out from a position of vulnerability and ask for support. Often, just as one is about to, a crisis comes along, and we go back to the "day-to-day" survival mentality, and the armor of invincibility goes back on. How can we better share our striving as human beings?

Collaborative research is an attempt to address these and other school issues. Collaboration means to work together, doing what any single one of us could not do alone. If one really means this then collaboration is not just a matter of sharing "results," but must characterize *each stage* of the research process. How can one be realistic, given the limitations of time and resources (see first section) and yet do research together? Is it possible to envision a model that is simple and yet multifaceted, one that does not take too much organizing and yet addresses other social and spiritual issues in the lives of teachers?

One clue comes from the traditions of oral history. Describing a collective project of residents of Hackney in East London, Thompson (1978) reports the interviews of community members and their lives with the intent of giving "back to people their own history, on the one hand, to build up through a series of individual accounts a composite history of life and work in Hackney, and, on the other, to give people confidence in their own memories of the past, their ability to contribute to the writing of history—confidence, in their own words: in short, in themselves."[30] In olden times, people would sit around the fireplace on a cold winter evening and tell stories—tales that would be passed down from one generation to the other. There was a thread of continuity here, and the group or family found its identity reflected in the oral traditions. The "bard" or storyteller of olden times has been replaced in most modern living rooms with flat panel TVs that do not serve the same purpose. We need to re-create cultural traditions and rituals more consciously if we are to hold on to our humanity. Re-searching and re-telling what one has found is one way to re-awaken human connections.

The above-mentioned project involving the creation of an oral history reminded me that adults learn best from each other and through sharing experiences.

This awareness has helped me formulate the following model for collaborative research:

A. Hearing questions

I suggest that at an early faculty meeting in the fall, a substantial portion of the afternoon be devoted to the sharing of questions as described earlier in this text. One might begin by asking that each teacher take ten minutes to quietly write down her/his "wonderings." Then divide the faculty into groups of three to share. The two members of each group that are listening would see themselves as coaches, first asking their colleague what kind of feedback would help, then perhaps asking questions for clarification, helping find connections between the wonderings, and in general, encourage. The roles in the small groups would then switch. At the end of the small-group sessions, each teacher should affirm the feedback received and choose one question that is of greatest importance. This coaching stage needs at least an hour. Then the faculty could reconvene, and the chair needs to set the tone with a few words about their "circle of trust" and the spirit in which questions are shared. This might make it possible for each teacher to share a question that could serve as a companion for the school year, a question that has enough passion to enthuse commitment.

Example question: How can teachers best meet the learning and developmental needs of boys?

B. Finding a Structure for Questions

Much time can be saved if the research process is looked at from the viewpoint of methodology at this early point. I suggest that we look to the education departments of interested universities to provide research consultants to visit the schools that have undertaken this project and meet with colleagues individually to draw up an outline of how, when and where the research will be conducted. Some things could be demonstrated in a large-group setting such as the faculty meeting, but other issues are really individual, and the methods used in research must suit the particular question. By having, say, the same consultant visit several schools, he or she could help teachers from different schools connect, based on shared interests. This "research web" would gradually provide a new layer of "association."

Example: Pose the question about boys at a faculty meeting, a teachers' conference or a family gathering, and ask participants to voluntarily fill out a questionnaire that you will leave on the table. Be willing to do this for other people's projects.

C. *Following a Question*

This stage involves data collection, as described above. I suggest that the faculty again find small groups to serve as a monthly "check-in," at which time each member would expect to hear an update on the progress. The importance here is not approval or even feedback, but rather staying with the task and reporting on progress. Support listening is crucial. This process is very much part of learning. As stated by Jon Wagner, "Research itself is a form of learning, and research reporting a form of teaching."[31]

Example: Do diary entries on your classroom observations of boys and how they respond in different classes.

D. Collegial Review

About half way through the year, each teacher could write a brief three-to-five page narrative, describing the project—a sort of overview. This narrative would be shared in the cohort group of three and sent to the research consultant for review. This collegial review, if handled rightly, can be tremendously affirming, lessen the stress issues around research, and enhance the social life within a school through shared interests. The responses from peers could be gathered and used as an assessment tool.

Example: Present some preliminary findings on the question of boys' development at a gathering of peers and ask for feedback. The responses will inform you about how you are communicating and what resonates with other teachers.

E. The Symposium

I envision that in the spring there could be a festive symposium, in which three to four schools could hold a weekend conference to share some of their research projects. I suggest that the host school not be one that has done the collaborative research, so that the presenters are free to focus on their sharing. Each school should send the topics proposed for the conference to the research consultant, who would group them thematically. Also, some teachers might need to be dissuaded or encouraged. The consultant could also serve as the convener at the weekend conference, setting the tone for presentations to follow. Proceedings could occasionally be published; thus helping to change the often one-sided focus of the media on testing and outcome-based assessment.

Example: Present a more formal "paper" on how teachers today are meeting the needs of boys. Distribute evaluation forms afterwards. Use them as part of your analysis.

I suggest that each presentation be no more than twenty to thirty minutes, the distilled essence of a year's work. The inner activity in this process of winnowing can be rewarding for the presenter and helps keep the audience focused. One might have three to four such presentations around a common theme, preceded by speech or singing. After each cluster, I suggest a short break and then discussion groups that would look at themes arising from the reports and provide a vehicle for questions to the presenters, and thus the recapitulation of the entire process that began with questions. One might have one group of presentations on Friday evening, one each on Saturday morning, Saturday afternoon and Sunday morning. The conference could end with a plenum of "the research process," thus allowing for the rewrite of this book.

This symposium format, with the feedback mechanism built into the structure, also allows for a response to the Heisenberg Effect—the uncertainty principle—which might cause some to question the accuracy of any study, since the observer/researcher may have affected the results by simply being a part of the equation.[32] One of the best ways to check up on ourselves and our biases is to share the results with the informants (those who participated) and our colleagues. Teachers know when something rings true or needs modification. Our colleagues are our best recourse in dealing with the uncertainty principle.

Please note what is not included in the above: antiseptic methods, a long research paper, onerous deadlines, and lots of extracurricular activities. Teachers already do much of what has been described. They go to conferences, read, meet, share, and so on. Simply use the venues already available—just put research sharing on the table for all to partake. This collaborative model is mainly an intensification of teacher preparation, with an eye towards forming a research community.

If possible, the proceedings of the symposium should be recorded, a transcript made, edited and then made available to teachers in other regions of North America. Over time, with alternating regions taking this up, a considerable body of primary material would become available to the parents and teachers alike. Even before then, however, the social/transformative benefits would be felt in our schools. Over time, some of the concerns expressed in the first two chapters of this book would be addressed; teachers would have a greater "voice" in educational decision making, policy might focus more on the real needs of children, and the government might back off when the vitality of the profession is experienced in one community after another. After all, who elects our political leaders anyway? Steven Montgomery from the Waldorf Teacher Education Program at Antioch New England states it thus:

> The activity of research serves two important functions: 1) As an exploration in more depth of questions and thoughts which seem important to our individual growth and inner purpose, and 2) as it results in a movement forward to

communicate to others what stirs our deepest human interest. This process of articulation is essential to participating actively in the social realm."

12. WHY DO RESEARCH?
(REVISITED)

SPIRITUAL DEVELOPMENT

IN THIS SECTION I would like to touch on a few themes, indicating areas that might prove fruitful to those looking at the research process as a matter of self-development.

Here are a few themes:

RESEARCH AS A PATH OF KNOWLEDGE

How can I learn what I need to know in order to teach? This question is a constant companion to many a teacher. Learning and teaching walk side by side down the path of life; the one is inseparable from the other. Learning through "preparation" and learning through teaching inform one another; they create the rich tapestry we call experience.

The demands of the profession are such, however, that many teachers move from one four-course meal to another; they learn the content needed in the immediate situation, but often have little time to process the experiences. Even though the content worked with may be rich, the preparation methods all too often consist of academic habits carried over from the teacher's own undergraduate years.

How can teachers renew the art of learning? One approach is to reexamine the process of knowing, to re-search.

In the book *The Stages of Higher Knowledge*, Rudolf Steiner describes four phases or steps in the path of knowledge:

1. Material Knowledge
2. Imaginative Knowledge
3. Inspirational Knowledge
4. Intuitive Knowledge[33]

I would like to use this sequence to indicate how research can enhance spiritual development and intensify the process of teacher preparation. In the Waldorf model, teachers are asked to move from grade to grade, following a group of children. This necessitates a great deal of new preparation each year. It is not enough to just amass large amounts of information—good teachers learn how to process the material and transform it in age-appropriate, exciting ways, designing activities and learning experiences that awaken the curiosity and passion of their students. In order to do this "awakening," the teacher herself must be inwardly alive. Imagination, inspiration and a healthy dose of intuition go a long way in the teaching profession.

In the course of a day we take in many sense impressions. These impressions come from objects and things around us in everyday life. Yet these sensations are meaningless without a response. We respond to the impression with our feelings, a part of our supersensible organism called the sentient soul. In the meeting of outer sensation and soul response, consciousness is born. One can then turn away from the original sense impressions and, because of the inner activity involved in the response, an image remains. We can then "make sense" of the image by forming a "concept" out of the original image. For example, one might see a clipper ship in the harbor on July 4th, retain the image even when one turns away, but it is only when one forms the concept "ship" that one has achieved understanding. But a fourth element enters the process of material cognition, namely the organizing element of the ego. Through its activity, images and concepts are united and form the basis of memory. The image itself remains only as long as the soul is engaged in the sensory experience, but thanks to the ego, we are able to relate the impressions of today with those of the past; we are able to remember. This is the foundation of our inner life.

Also in regard to concepts, the ego engages in relational activity. It combines concepts, builds understanding, and through marvelous inner activity, helps the human being form judgments. Thus material cognition is based upon the ability to process sensations so that an image is formed, a concept arises, and is unified by the activity of the ego. The act of cognition is the basic building block of research.

At the next, higher level of cognition, the sensation from without is replaced by an image from within. This is called *imagination*. Through this faculty, images can become active for the individual that are not dependent upon physical sensation, but can be nevertheless just as vivid and true. Through meditation and other exercises one can gradually learn to form meaningful images free of sensory stimulation. Yet the process of forming concepts and the relatedness achieved by the ego remain just as important, if not more so, than before, in that one has to learn to discern real images from flights of fancy. When working with imaginative cognition, the responsibility of the researcher becomes all the greater.

In the third stage, image no longer plays a role, for now one is working just with "concept" and "ego." The human being lives wholly within the spiritual world. The stimulation of sensation in the first stage is replaced by *imagination* in the second, and *inspiration* in the third stage of cognition. One is able to actually hear the tones of the spiritual world and penetrate to the very heart of things. This is what is happening, for example, when one wakes up one morning and says, "Now I know what book I will give Ben to read."

And finally, in the fourth stage, the ego remains alone. The experience, as related by Rudolf Steiner, is that of no longer being outside things and occurrences, but now one stands within them. This living into things is called *intuition*. Then, when one is in the middle of a busy classroom, with little time for consideration of planning, suddenly one takes action, intervenes in a social situation among the children, and afterwards one wonders, "Where did that come from?"

Although this book has dealt mainly with techniques on the first level of knowing, material cognition, it seems essential to describe the full process available to the student of higher knowledge. For research and self-development are, in my opinion, vitally connected. The results achieved at one level can only be fructified and enhanced by the striving of another level of insight.

In working with the above passages, it occurred to me that those engaged in research have, especially in recent years, articulated numerous avenues of inquiry that somewhat parallel the four stages just described. So for instance, heuristic research attempts to get inside of the experience. Qualitative research accepts the role of intuition getting to the essence of the questions. Phenomenology accepts the importance of both outer and inner events as in the second stage, and traditional, quantitative research places an emphasis on what is linked to sense perceptions.

Depending upon the subject of the inquiry, those engaged in research are advised to consider not only the content but also the process that is most suitable. Do we want to look at things from the outside or from the inside? In everyday life, one usually experiences the world from outside and oneself from the inside. Research contains the possibility, if necessary, of reversing this: to experience things as if from the inside and oneself as if from outside. Knowledge of the world thus goes hand in hand with knowledge of self. And how we get there is just as important as what we find. As Emily Bowers from the Waldorf Teacher Education Program at Antioch New England says, "While I have long had a deep love and connection with the French language, my research enabled me to penetrate the 'genius of the language.' With a better understanding of the development of the French language, I came upon the greater revelation of the evolution of human speech—speech in its highest glory and darkest hour."

One also has to start somewhere. So often teachers shy away from even the thought of research, and thus I have tried to address research on a simple, "first steps" basis, in the hopes that some new activity is stimulated. Part of the challenge is simply organizing ourselves, learning how to ask the question, observe, collect and share. But I hope the process is both internal and external; that self-development goes hand in hand with strengthening connections between schools and teachers. A research collaborative can do for education what farmers' markets have done for local villages in New England. We need to grow our standards organically rather than importing solutions that don't fit. Sharing teacher research projects can help educators be proactive in setting the agenda rather than always responding to outside mandates. A community of enthusiastic teachers can bring back a sense of neighborhood schools and of community. A stronger voice for the local community will push back against state and federal legislation. And in the end, the only ones "left behind" may be the old-style politicians who care more about their campaign donations than about the needs of real children. The best thing about democracy is the possibility of civic action. It is time for teachers and parents to speak out, for they know what their children need most.

13. RESEARCH AS
TEACHER EMPOWERMENT

THIS IS A natural result of the research process. As we intensify our observations, gain understanding as well as self-knowledge, reflect on practice and learn to better articulate what we are doing, we can experience a new kind of professional and personal freedom. This can lead to new roles in educational leadership and community activism as described earlier.

RESEARCH AS RENEWAL

One might simply take up the theme of stress transformation. Find something that bothers you, and make it your research question. It is amazing what happens when a source of frustration is brought under observation and study for a period of time. When I became concerned about teacher burnout, I started to observe the phenomena in myself and in others, and I finally took it up as a research project that culminated in my second book, *School Renewal.*

RESEARCH AND PROFESSIONAL DEVELOPMENT

If we as teachers are actively engaged in learning through research, our students benefit immediately. Our involvement, even if not on grade level material, acts as a quickening element in their learning. Our vitality and enthusiasm directly affects the participation and health of the children. In the schools I have observed, those teachers who are "fired up," enthusiastic and engaging are often those who are most actively engaged in the discovery process themselves. They are seeing things with "new eyes" and bringing a fresh simplicity to their work with children.

RESEARCH AS A DEEPENING OF EDUCATION

On September 6, 1919, at the end of his address to the teachers of the first Waldorf school in Stuttgart, Rudolf Steiner called attention to something that he wanted to lay upon the hearts of the teachers present. These simple principles are as important for teachers today as they were back in 1919:

> The teacher must be a person of initiative in
>   everything he or she does, great and small.
> The teacher should be one who is interested in
>   the being of the whole world and of humanity.
> The teacher must be one who never makes a
>   compromise in his or her heart and mind with
>   what is untrue.
> The teacher must never get stale or grow sour.[34]

If one lives with these four statements and the text that accompanies them in a book called the *Deepening of Waldorf Education*, one cannot but see the relevance of teacher-inspired research.

Teachers now need to take initiative, become "authors" in the larger sense. Research affords us an opportunity to accept the challenge of the age of the consciousness soul, pass through the eye of the needle, and come through our experiences as individuals who speak with a new voice. This next stage of our work is not a luxury; it is a necessity if we are to counter NCLB and other government mandates. The creative forces that may be released from enchantment, if teacher research is truly taken up, cannot be fully imagined. It all begins with the response of each individual to this call. Let me end with a passage from *Leaves of Grass* by Walt Whitman:

> You shall no longer take things at second or third
>   hand,
> Nor look through the eyes of the dead, nor feed
>   on the specters of books,
> You shall not look through my eyes either, nor
>   take things from me,
> You shall listen to all sides and filter them from
>   yourself.[35]

APPENDIX*

ALTERNATIVE QUESTION FORMATS

Dichotomous lead-in questions	Presupposition lead-in questions
Do you feel like you know enough about the program to assess its effectiveness?	How effective do you think the program is? (Presupposes that a judgment can be made)
Have you learned anything from this program?	What have you learned from this program? (Presupposes learning)
Do you do anything now in your work that you didn't do before the program began?	What do you do now that you didn't do before the program began? (Presupposes change)
Is there any misuse of funds in this program?	What kinds of misuse of funds have occurred in this program? (Presupposes at least some misuse of funds)
Are there any conflicts among the staff?	What kinds of staff conflicts have occurred here? (Presupposes conflicts)

* Special thanks to Michael Patton for much of the material in this appendix.

Fieldwork Strategies
and Observation Methods

I. Role of the Evaluator-Observer

Full   **Onlooker**

Participant observation	Partial observation	Observation as an outsider

II. Portrayal of the Evaluator Role to Others

Overt   **Covert**

Observations: Program staff and participants know that observations are being made or who the observer is	Observer: Role known by some, not by others	Observations: Program staff and participants do not know that others are present as observers

III. Portrayal of the Purpose of the Evaluation to Others

Full explanation of real purpose to everyone	Partial explanations	Covert explanations: None given to either staff or participants	False explanations: Staff and particpants deceived about evaluation purpose

IV. Duration of the Evaluation Observations

Single observation: Limited duration (e.g., one hour)	Long-term, multiple observations (e.g., months, years)

V. Focus of the Observations

Narow focus   **Broad Focus**

Single element or component in the program observed	Holistic view of the entire program and all of its elements

INTERVIEWS

ACTUAL INTERVIEW:	WHAT THE INTERVIEWER REALLY WANTED TO KNOW: OPEN-ENDED QUESTION:
Q: Were you the evaluator of this program?	What was your role in this program?
A: Yes.	
Q: Were you doing a formative evaluation?	What was the purpose of the evaluation?
A: Mostly.	
Q: Were you trying to find out if the people changed from being in the wilderness?	What were you trying to find out in doing the evaluation?
A: That was part of it.	
Q: Did they change?	How did participation in the program affect participants?
A: Some of them did.	
Q: Did you interview people both before and after the program?	What kinds of information did you collect for the evaluation?
A: Yes.	
Q: Did you also go along as a participant in the program?	How were you personally involved in the program?
A: Yes.	
Q: Did you find that being in the program affected what happened?	How do you think your participation in the program affected what happened?
A: Yes.	
Q: Did you have a good time?	What was the wilderness experience like for you?
A: Yes.	

Vague and Overgeneralized Notes:	Detailed and Concrete Notes:
1. The new client was uneasy waiting for her intake interview.	1. At first the new client sat very stiffly on the chair next to the receptionist's desk. She picked up a magazine and let the pages flutter through her fingers very quickly without really looking at any of the pages. She set the magazine down, looked at her watch, tugged at her skirt, and picked up the magazine again. This time she didn't look at the magazine. She set it back down, took out a cigarette, and began smoking. She would watch the receptionist out of the corner of her eye, and then look down at the magazine, and back up at the two or three other people waiting in the room. Her eyes moved from the people to the magazine to the cigarette to the people to the magazine in rapid succession. She avoided eye contact. When her name was finally called she jumped as if she was startled.
2. The client was quite hostile toward the staff person.	2. When Judy, the senior staff member, told her that she could not do what she wanted to do, the client began to yell at Judy, telling her that she couldn't control her life, that she was on nothing but a "power trip," that she'd "like to beat the shit out of her," and that she could just "go to hell." She shook her fist in Judy's face and stomped out of the room, leaving Judy standing there with her mouth open, looking amazed.
3. The next student who came in to take the test was very poorly dressed	3. The next student who came into the room was wearing clothes quite different from the three students who'd been in previously. The three previous students looked like they'd been groomed before they came to the test. Their hair was combed, their clothes were clean and pressed, the colors of their clothes matched, and their clothes were in good condition. This new student had on pants that were dirty, with a hole or tear in one knee and a threadbare seat. The flannel shirt was wrinkled, with one tail tucked into the pants and the other tail hanging out. His hair was disheveled, and his hands looked as though he'd been playing in the engine of a car.

VARIETY IN QUALITATIVE INQUIRY: THEORETICAL TRADITIONS

PERSPECTIVE:	DISCIPLINARY ROOTS:	CENTRAL QUESTIONS:
1. Ethnography	Anthropology	What is the culture of this group of people?
2. Phenomenology	Philosophy	What is the structure and essence of experience of this phenomenon for these people?
3. Heuristics	Humanistic psychology	What is my experience of this phenomenon and the essential experience of others who also experience this phenomenon intensely?
4. Ethnomethodology	Sociology	How do people make sense of their everyday activities so as to behave in socially acceptable ways?
5. Symbolic interactionism	Social psychology	What common set of symbols and understandings have emerged to give meaning to people's interactions?
6. Ecological psychology	Ecology, Psychology	How do individuals attempt to accomplish their goals through specific behaviors in specific environments?
7. Systems theory	Interdisciplinary	How and why does this system function as a whole?
8. Chaos theory: nonlinear interaction	Theoretical physics, Natural sciences	What is the underlying order, if any, of disorderly phenomenon?
9. Hermeneutics	Theology, Philosophy, Literary criticism	What are the conditions under which a human act took place or a product was produced that makes it possible to interpret its meanings?
10. Orientational, qualitative	Ideologies, Political economy	How is x ideological perspective manifest in this phenomenon?

Typology of Research Purposes

Types of Research	Purpose	Focus of Research	Desired Results
Basic research	Knowledge as an end in itself; discover truth	Questions deemed important by one's discipline or personal intellectual interest	Contribution to theory
Applied research	Understand the nature and sources of human and societal problems	Questions deemed important by society	Contributions to theory that can be used to formulate problem-solving programs and interventions
Summative evaluation	Determine effectiveness of human interventions and actions (programs, policies, personnel, and products)	Goals of intervention	Judgments and generalizations about effective types of interventions and the conditions under which those efforts are effective
Formative evaluation	Improve an intervention, a program, policy, organization, or product	Strengths and weaknesses of the specific program, policy, or personnel being studied	Recommendations for limited improvement
Action research	Solve problems in a program, organization, or community	Organization and community problems	Immediate action; solving problems as quickly as possible

⋯RED LEVEL OF ⋯ERALIZATION	KEY ASSUMPTIONS	PUBLICATION MODE	STANDARD FOR JUDGING
⋯oss time and ⋯ce (ideal)	The world is patterned; those patterns are knowable and explainable	Major refereed scholarly journals in one's discipline, scholarly books	Rigor of research, universality and verifiability of theory
⋯hin as ⋯eral a time ⋯ space as ⋯sible, but ⋯arly limited ⋯lication ⋯text	Human and societal problems can be understood and solved with knowledge	Specialized academic journals, applied research journals within disciplines, interdisciplinary problem-focused journals	Rigor and theoretical insight into the problem
⋯interventions ⋯ similar ⋯als	What works one place under specified conditions should work elsewhere	Evaluation reports for program funders and policy makers, specialized journals	Generalizability to future efforts and to other programs and policy issues
⋯ited to ⋯ecific setting ⋯died	People can and will use information to improve what they're doing	Oral briefings, conferences, internal report, limited circulation to similar programs, other evaluators	Usefulness to and actual use by intended users in the setting studied
⋯re and now	People in a setting can solve problems by studying themselves	Interpersonal Interactions among research participants; informal, unpublished	Feelings about the process among research participants, feasibility of the solution generated

SAMPLING STRATEGIES

TYPES	PURPOSES
A. Random probability sampling	Representativeness: Sample size a function of population size and desired confidence level.
1. simple random sample	Permits generalization from sample to the population it represents.
2. stratified random and cluster samples	Increases confidence in generalizing to particular subgroups or areas.
B. Purposeful sampling	Selects information-rich cases for in-depth study. Size and specific cases depend on study purpose.
1. extreme or deviant case sampling	Learning from highly unusual manifestations of the phenomenon of interest, such as outstanding successes/notable failures, top of the class/dropouts, exotic events, and crises.
2. intensity sampling	Information-rich cases that manifest the phenomenon intensely, but not extremely, such as good students/poor students, about average/below average.
3. maximum variation sampling—purposefully picking a wide range of variation on dimensions of interest	Documents unique or diverse variations that have emerged in adapting to different conditions. Identifies important common patterns that cut across variations.
4. homogeneous sampling	Focuses, reduces variation, simplifies analysis, and facilitates group interviewing.
5. typical case sampling	Illustrates or highlights what is typical, normal, and average.
6. stratified purposeful sampling	Illustrates characteristics of particular subgroups of interest; facilitates comparisons.

7. critical case sampling	Permits logical generalization and maximum application of information to other cases because if it's true of this one case, it's likely to be true of all other cases.
TYPES	**PURPOSES**
8. snowball or chain sampling	Identifies cases of interest from people who know people who know people who know what cases are information-rich, that is, good examples for study, good interview subjects.
9. criterion sampling	Picking all cases that meet some criterion, such as all children abused in a treatment facility. Quality assurance.
10. theory-based or operational construct sampling	Finding manifestations of a theoretical construct of interest to elaborate and examine the construct.
11. confirming and disconfirming cases	Elaborating and deepening initial analysis, seeking exceptions, testing variation.
12. opportunistic sampling	Following new leads during fieldwork, taking advantage of the unexpected, flexibility.
13. random purposeful sampling (still small sample size)	Adds credibility to sample when potential purposeful sample is larger than one can handle. Reduces judgment within a purposeful category (not for generalizations or representations).
14. sampling politically important cases	Attracts attention to the study (or avoids attracting undesired attention by purposefully eliminating from the sample politically sensitive cases).
15. convenience sampling	Saves time, money, and effort. Poorest rationale; lowest credibility. Yields information-poor cases.
16. combination or mixed purposeful sampling	Triangulation, flexibility, meets multiple interests and needs.

DESIGN ISSUES AND OPTIONS

ISSUES	SAMPLE OPTIONS AND CONSIDERATIONS
1. What is the primary purpose of the study?	Basic research, applied research, summative evaluation, formative evaluation, action research.
2. What is the focus of the study?	Breadth versus depth trade-offs.
3. What are the units of analysis?	Individuals, groups, program components, whole programs, organizations, communities, critical incidents, time periods, and so on.
4. What will be the sampling strategy or strategies?	Purposeful sampling, probability sampling; variations in sample size from a single case study to generalizable samples.
5. What types of data will be collected?	Qualitative, quantitative, or both.
6. What controls will be exercised?	Naturalistic inquiry, experimental design, quasi-experimental options.
7. What analytical approach or approaches will be used?	Inductive analysis, deductive content analysis, statistical analysis, combinations.

8. How will validity of and confidence in findings be addressed?	Triangulation options, multiple data sources, multiple methods, multiple perspectives, and multiple investigators.
9. Time issues: When will the study occur? How will the study be sequenced or phased?	Long-term fieldwork, rapid reconnaissance, exploratory phase to confirmatory phase, fixed times versus open time lines.
10. How will logistics and practicalities be handled?	Gaining entry to the setting, access to people and records, contracts, training, endurance, and so on.
11. How will ethical issues and matters of confidentiality be handled?	Informed consent, protection of human subjects, reactivity, presentation of self, and so on.
12. What resources will be available? What will the study cost?	Personnel, supplies, data collection, materials, analysis time and costs, reporting/publishing costs.

VARIATIONS IN INTERVIEW INSTRUMENTATION

TYPE OF INTERVIEW	CHARACTERISTICS
(1) Informal conversational approach	Questions emerge from the immediate context and are asked in the natural course of things; there is no predetermination of question topics in wording.
(2) Interview guide approach	Topics and issues to be covered are specified in advance in outline form; interviewer decides sequence and wording of questions in the course of the interview
(3) Standardized open-ended interview	The exact wording and sequence of questions are determined in advance. All interviewees are asked the same basic questions in the same order. Questions are worded in a completely open-ended format.
(4) Closed, fixed response interview	Questions and response categories are determined in advance. Responses are fixed; respondent chooses from among the fixed responses.

ʀᴇɴɢᴛʜs	Wᴇᴀᴋɴᴇssᴇs
₊reases the salience and relevance questions; interviews are built on and ₊erge from observations; the interview ₊n be matched to individuals and cumstances.	Different information collected from different people with different questions. Less systematic and comprehensive if certain questions do not arise "naturally." Data organization and analysis can be quite difficult.
e outline increases the ₊mprehensiveness of the data and ₊kes data collection somewhat ₊tematic for each respondent. ₊gical gaps in data can be anticipated ₊d closed. Interviews remain fairly ₊nversational and situational.	Important and salient topics may be inadvertently omitted. Interviewer flexibility in sequencing and wording questions can result in substantially different responses from different perspectives, thus reducing the comparability of responses.
₊spondents answer the same ₊estions, thus increasing comparability ₊responses; data are complete for each ₊rson on the topics addressed in the ₊erview. Reduces interviewer effects ₊d bias when several interviewers are ₊ed. Permits evaluation users to see ₊d review the instrumentation used in ₊e evaluation. Facilitates organization ₊d analysis of the data.	Little flexibility in relating the interview to particular individuals and circumstance; standardized wording of questions may constrain and limit naturalness and relevance of questions and answers.
₊ta analysis is simple; responses ₊n be directly compared and easily ₊gregated; many questions can be ₊ked in a short time.	Respondents must fit their experiences and feelings into the researcher's categories; may be perceived as impersonal, irrelevant, and mechanistic. Can distort what respondents really mean or experienced by so completely limiting their response choices.

Notes

1. Thomas B. Fordham Institute: The Education Gadfly, www.edexcellence.netfoundation.gadfly.index.cfm/#3177.
2. Education Policy Analysis Archives, http://epaa.asu.edu/epaa/v14n23.
3. *Educational Leadership*, November 2006, Vol. 64, No. 3, 10.
4. Fordham Institute, 4.
5. Fordham Institute, 4.
6. Susan Ohanian, *One Size Fits Few: The Folly of Educational Standards*. (Portsmouth: Heinemann Publishing, 1999), 4.
7. Ibid., 150.
8. John Gardner, *Freedom and the Independent School*, (Washington, DC: Myrin Institute, 1976).
9. Rudolf Steiner, *The Renewal of the Social Organism*, (New York: Anthroposophic Press, 1985), 73.
10. Rudolf Steiner, *The Renewal of the Social Organism*, 75.
11. Glenda Bissex, from a guest appearance at Antioch New England, 1994.
12. David Hopkins, *A Teacher's Guide to Classroom Research*, (Salisbury, UK: Open University Press, 1985), 29.

13. Power and Hubbard, *Teacher Research: The Journal of Classroom Inquiry*, (Albany, NY: The Johnson Press, 1994, Vol. 1), 72.

14. David Hopkins, *A Teacher's Guide to Classroom Research*, 33.

15. Power and Hubbard, *Teacher Research*, 67.

16. David Hopkins, *A Teacher's Guide to Classroom Research*, 48.

17. David Hopkins, 3.

18. Michael Patton, *Qualitative Evaluation and Research Methods*, (New York: Sage Publications, 1990).

19. Power and Hubbard, *Teacher Research*, 79.

20. Theodore Sizer, *Horace's Compromise*, (Boston: Houghton Mifflin Co., 1985), 99–100.

21. David Hopkins, *A Teacher's Guide to Classroom Research*, 46.

22. Power and Hubbard, *Teacher Research*, 75.

23. Jon Wagner, "Ignorance in Educational Research Or, How Can You Not Know That?," In *Educational Research*, Vol. 22, No 5, 15–23.

24. Harry F. Wolcott, *Writing up Qualitative Research*, (London: Sage Publications, 1990), 31.

25. Power and Hubbard, *Teacher Research*, 82.

26. Harry F. Wolcott, *Writing Up Qualitative Research*, 35–39.

27. Patton, 150.

28. Laurel Richardson, *Writing, A Method of Inquiry, Handbook of Qualitative Research*, Denizin and Lincoln, (London: Sage Publications, 1994), 516.

29. Harry F. Wolcott, *Writing Up Qualitative Research*, 21.

30. Elliot G. Mishler, *Research Interviewing: Context and Narrative*, 15.

31. Jon Wagner, *Educational Research*, 20.

32. Power and Hubbard, *Teacher Research*, 74.

33. Rudolf Steiner, *The Stages of Higher Knowledge*, (Hudson, New York: Anthroposophic Press, 1967), 4–10.

34. Rudolf Steiner, *Towards the Deepening of Waldorf Education*, (Forest Row, Sussex, UK: The Steiner Schools Fellowship Pub., 1977), 26–27.

35. Walt Whitman, *Leaves of Grass*, (New York: Signet Classic, New American Library, 1955), 50.

BIBLIOGRAPHY

BOOKS

Argyrris, Chris. *Knowledge For Action*. San Francisco: Jossey-Bass Publishers, 1993.

Creswell, John. *Research Design, Qualitative & Quantitative Approaches*. Thousand Oaks: Sage Publications, 1994.

Friere, Paulo. *Pedagogy of the Oppressed*. New York: Continuum Publishing, 1990.

Hopkins, David. *A Teacher's Guide to Classroom Research*. Philadelphia: Open University Press, 1985.

Shagoury Hubbard, Ruth, and Brenda Miller Power. *The Art of Classroom Inquiry: A Handbook for Teacher-Researches*. Portsmouth, NH: Heinemann, 1993.

Gardner, John Fentress. *Towards A Truly Public Education: A Philosophy of Independence for Schools*. New York: The Myrin Institute, 1966.

Gardner, John Fentress. *The Next Step*. New York: The Myrin Institute, 1975.

Gardner, John Fentress. *Freedom and the Independent School*. New York: The Myrin Institute, 1975.

Gardner, John Fentress. *Freedom for Education*. New York: The Myrin Institute, 1975.

Mishler, Elliot G. *Research Interviewing: Context and Narrative*. Cambridge, MA: Harvard University Press, 1991.

Ohanian, Susan. *One Size Fits Few: The Folly of Educational Standards*. Portsmouth, NH: Heinemann Publishing, 1999.

Patton, Michael Quinn. *Qualitative Evaluation and Research Methods*. New Delhi: Sage Publications, 1990.

Stoff, Sheldon P. *Freedom and Independence in Education*. Washington, DC: Council for Educational Freedom in America, 1977.

Steiner, Rudolf. *Towards the Deepening of Waldorf Education*. Dornach, Switzerland: Pedagogical Section of The School of Spiritual Science, 1991.

Steiner, Rudolf. *The Social Future*. Great Barrington, MA: Anthroposophic Press, 1972.

Steiner, Rudolf. *The Renewal of the Social Organism*. Great Barrington, MA: Anthroposophic Press, 1985.

Wolcott, Harry F. *Writing Up Qualitative Research*. New Delhi: Sage Publications, 1990.

JOURNALS AND INTERNET SOURCES

Educational Leadership, November 2006, vol. 64, no 3.

"Thomas B. Fordham Institute: The Education Gadfly," www.edexcellence.net/foundation/gadfly/index. cfm#3177.

The Research Bulletin, Research Institute for Waldorf Education, autumn 2006, vol. xii, no. 1.

Research Institute
for Waldorf Education

THE RESEARCH INSTITUTE FOR WALDORF EDUCATION is an initiative working on behalf of the Waldorf school movement. The Institute was founded in 1996 in order to deepen and enhance the quality of Waldorf education, to engage in serious and sustained dialogue with the wider educational-cultural community, and to support research that would serve educators in all types of schools in their work with children and adolescents.

The Research Institute supports research projects that deal with essential contemporary educational issues such as attention-related disorders, trends in adolescent development, innovations in the high school curriculum, learning expectations and assessment, computers in education, the role of art in education, and new ways to identify and address different learning styles. The Research Institute has sponsored colloquia and conferences that have brought together educators, psychologists, doctors, and social scientists. The Institute publishes a *Research Bulletin* twice a year, and we develop and distribute educational resources to help teachers in all aspects of their work, through the On-Line Waldorf Library at www.waldorflibrary.org.

The Research Institute receives financial support through the Association of Waldorf Schools of North America (AWSNA), the Midwest Shared Gifting Group, the Waldorf Schools Fund, the Waldorf Curriculum Fund, the Waldorf Educational Foundation, as well as private donors. The Research Institute is a 501(c) (3) tax-exempt organization and gratefully accepts donations.

Douglas Gerwin and David Mitchell, Co-Directors
P.O. Box 307, Wilton, NH 03086
Phone: (603) 654-2566 • Fax: (603) 654-5258
www.waldorfresearchinstitute.org

Center for Anthroposophy

Waldorf Teacher Education & Renewal

Working out of the science of the spirit pioneered by Rudolf Steiner, the Center for Anthroposophy offers innovative adult education programs that:

- Stimulate new inner growth and development
- Transform existing gifts and talents into creative capacities
- Re-enliven life's experiences so that they become seeds for research and future work in the world

Located in Wilton, New Hamphire, the Center supports schools worldwide by continually renewing Waldorf teachers and those who stand with them as administrators, trustees, parents, and friends.

Waldorf High School
Teacher Education Program
Douglas Gerwin, Program Chair
A graduate level program leading to a Waldorf high school teaching certificate in:
Arts/Art History – English – History – Life Sciences – Mathematics –
Physical Sciences – Pedagogical Eurythmy

Foundation Studies
in Anthroposophy and the Arts
Barbara Richardson, Coordinator
A program combining basic anthroposophical principles and self-development exercises with artistic experiences that lay the groundwork for those exploring the foundations of Waldorf education, or seeking to become Waldorf teachers.

Renewal Courses
Karine Munk Finser, Coordinator
An annual series of five-day summer retreats bringing together Waldorf teachers and others for personal rejuvenation and social renewal through anthroposophical study, artistic immersion, good food and fun.

Research
Provides opportunities for individual teachers or teams of researchers to undertake research projects concerning Waldorf education in the fields of curriculum, child development, governance, adult education, parent relations, etc.

Center for Anthroposophy
(603) 654-2566
For a complete listing of courses please visit
www.centerforanthroposophy.org

CPSIA information can be obtained
at www.ICGtesting.com
Printed in the USA
FFOW02n1042160718
47403692-50561FF